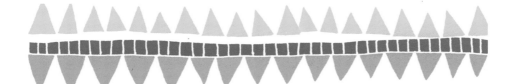

YOUNG, GIFTED AND BLACK, TOO

WIDE EYED EDITIONS

CONTENTS

WELCOME (TO) THIS BOOK!

The team that brought you *Young, Gifted and Black* is back with much love and appreciation to the next generation. We bring you a celebration of 52 MORE icons whose stories are waiting over the pages to be discovered.

We remain inspired by the song "To be Young, Gifted and Black," which iconic singer Nina Simone wrote as a tribute to her friend Lorraine Hansberry, the first Black woman to write a Broadway play.

Since the song was initially performed in 1969, it has been covered and sampled by many artists who have uniquely made it their own and, in a way, issued an invitation to the next generation to follow in the tradition of taking inspiration and motivation from the heroes who came before them.

What do heroes inspire you to make or do with your own gifts?

We welcome new readers, and those familiar with the series, on a journey of discovery, a tour of the world, and an adventure through time to meet Black artists, activists, dreamers, doers, makers, athletes, healers, leaders, thinkers, and inventors. All children deserve to read positive stories of heroes like them, and we hope this book makes you feel celebrated, hopeful, connected, seen, and part of a global community, wherever you are.

In this book, our icons are ordered chronologically, showcasing Black achievement from the 1500s right up to present-day. Each biography is a snapshot of these incredible figures' rich lives, and we hope you feel moved to investigate and discover more, beyond the book.

As you turn each page, meet familiar faces, and learn about new remarkable heroes from around the world, ask yourself if you see yourself in some of their dreams, achievements, challenges, experiences, and curiosities.

How do you plan to write your name on the present and future pages?

Although our icons from past and present illustrate a myriad of different ways to live, work, love, and light up the world, they were and are in many ways just like you; singular, unique, incomparable, and themselves. Thank you for being perfectly and irreplaceably you.

You are one of our heroes, too.

Jamia Wilson & Andrea Pippins

JAMIA WILSON

ANDREA PIPPINS

Juan's remarkable mastery of Latin earned him the name "Juan Latino."

JUAN LATINO
(C. 1518-C. 1594)

Poet, professor, and self-described "teacher of the young," Juan de Sessa was the first Afro-Spaniard to publish a book in Latin verse in 1573.

Juan was born in around 1518 and was enslaved to a noble Spanish family for much of his life. As a child, Juan had a thirst for knowledge. He accompanied his enslaver's son Gonzalo to school, carrying Gonzalo's books and sitting in on classes. Juan's intelligence was noticed, and he was soon allowed to take part. He impressed his teachers with his brilliance and talent for Latin, Greek, and writing poetry.

After school, Juan went on to study at the University of Granada, earning a Bachelor of Arts degree in 1546. Juan then fell in love with and married a Spanish noblewoman. Their union was one of Spain's first legally recognized mixed-race partnerships.

Juan's achievements didn't stop there. He became a lecturer at the University of Granada and spent 20 years teaching students grammar and Latin. Juan also wrote and published three volumes of Latin poetry, including his epic poem, *Austrias Carmen*. He is remembered for his rich, boundary-breaking life.

QUEEN NANNY
(C. 1686–C. 1733)

Queen Nanny led the Maroons, a community of formerly enslaved Africans in Jamaica, in a fight for freedom from slavery and British colonial rule. Notorious for her rebellion and use of clever guerilla tactics, Nanny saw her enemies defeated time and time again.

In Nanny's time, many African people were transported to colonies in the Americas, where they were forced to work on plantations. Nanny was part of a group who had escaped enslavement and formed settlements high in the Blue Mountains of Jamaica. Nanny united her community and fought to stay free. She organized raids on plantations and battles against British troops. Her warriors knew the land, and would lay in wait, striking their enemies with precision. It's thought that Nanny's leadership and strategies helped free hundreds of enslaved people. Tired of losing, the British eventually negotiated with the Maroons, agreeing to their demands for free settlements.

Queen Nanny's role in the Maroons' resistance has been remembered and passed down in oral history for centuries. She is known as "The Mother of All Jamaicans," and remains an enduring symbol of resistance.

JAMAICA

Nanny's portrait appears on the Jamaican $500 note

TOUSSAINT L'OUVERTURE

(C. 1743-1803)

Celebrated as "the Father of Haiti," Toussaint L'Ouverture was a notorious leader in the fight for freedom from slavery and colonial rule. His legendary leadership paved the way for Haiti's establishment as the first free state founded by enslaved people.

Toussaint was born into slavery on the Breda plantation in Saint-Domingue (known today as Haiti), a French colony on the western section of the Caribbean Island of Hispaniola. Toussaint and other enslaved people lived there in captivity under white minority rule.

Toussaint was a talented person. He learned to read and write and, in addition to Haitian Creole and the African tribal language he spoke, he learned French and Latin. He was given extra responsibilities on the Breda plantation farm and was known for his skills training horses and working with medicinal plants. In his early thirties Toussaint gained his freedom and got married.

For almost 20 years, he raised his children with his wife Suzanne and worked as a paid steward and coachman on the plantation.

In 1791, there was a slave revolt and Toussaint felt convinced to join the struggle. He proved his worth as a soldier and leader, training, organizing, and recruiting formerly enslaved people. He famously declared: "Unite yourselves to us, brothers, and fight with us for the same cause."

First, he allied with the Spanish who controlled the other side of Hispaniola. Then, in 1794 when the French abolished slavery, he switched sides and fought the Spanish, seizing control of the whole of Hispaniola. Though Saint-Domingue was still a French colony, Toussaint was leading it, and in 1801 he declared a new constitution (a set of principles and laws) for the island that made him governor-general for the rest of his life.

The French grew wary of his power. In 1802, they arrested Toussaint and sent him to prison, where he died in 1803. A year later, resistance forces resumed the fight, and won, declaring Saint Domingue an independent nation named Haiti.

Famous for finding openings in his enemies' defences, Toussaint adopted the surname "L'Ouverture," meaning "the opening" in French.

CHEVALIER DE SAINT-GEORGES (1745-1799)

The first classical composer of African descent in Europe, Joseph de Bologne (AKA Chevalier de Saint-Georges) lived an exceptional life. He was a champion fencer, masterful composer, celebrated violinist, and all-round trailblazer.

Born in Guadeloupe, a then French colony, to a wealthy white father and a Black enslaved mother, Joseph was later taken to France where he studied and spent most of his life.

Joseph faced hardship: rivals mocked his heritage, French laws limited his freedoms, and he lost out on opportunities due to racism. Despite these obstacles, he persisted. He served as a colonel of an all-Black regiment during the French Revolution, he traveled, made music, and conducted famous and renowned orchestras. He was admired by many during his life and continues to inspire today.

Joseph was dubbed "the most talented man in Europe" by US President John Adams.

OLAUDAH EQUIANO (C. 1745-1797)

Olaudah Equiano made history for penning the first known major autobiographical book about an enslaved person's life. He exposed the brutality of slavery and helped garner support for the abolitionist movement in the United Kingdom.

At just 11 years old Olaudah was kidnapped from his home in modern-day Benin and enslaved. He was transported to the West Indies and Virginia then sold to a British ship commander. He was sold twice more before he bought his freedom in 1766. He settled in England and, in 1789, he published his book, *The Interesting Narrative of the Life of Olaudah Equiano*. He spent the rest of his life speaking up about the inhuman cruelty of slavery. His work helped inspire the 1807 British Slave Trade Act, bringing an end to the slave trade.

" My life had lost its relish when liberty was gone. "

ALEXANDER PUSHKIN

(1799-1837)

Alexander Pushkin was a poet, novelist, and playwright. He remains one of Russia's most famous writers, with many of his works translated around the world.

Alexander was the great-grandson of a military leader and governor named Gannibal, who had been kidnapped as a child from Cameroon, Africa. Gannibal's enslavers gave him to the Tsar of Russia, Peter the Great, who then freed and adopted him.

Born into the Tsar's inner circle, Alexander studied multiple languages, especially French. As a child, he enjoyed reading, meeting with his parents' visitors, and talking with local workers for hours on end. One of his nurses, Arina, shared folktales that later inspired his poems and his famous novel *Eugene Onegin*.

After his schooling, Alexander began to write about a fairer world for workers. His poem "Ode to Liberty" was a favorite among rebels who fought for social change. This angered Tsar Alexander I, who exiled Alexander to a distant part of Russia in punishment.

Despite this, Alexander persisted in writing until his death and is remembered as one of the greatest literary figures in history.

I was not born to amuse the Tsars.

YAA ASANTEWAA (1840-1921)

Yaa Asantewaa was a warrior queen in the Asante Empire (part of present-day southern Ghana) who led a fierce resistance against the British invasion and occupation of her people's lands.

Born to farmer parents, Yaa Asantewaa was the eldest of two children. Her name follows a tradition of naming children after the day they were born: girls born on a Thursday ("Yawoda" in Akan) are often named "Yaa."

As she came of age, Yaa studied cultural traditions, developed a skill for farming, sang in family and sacred rituals, sculpted clay objects, and worshipped at her family shrine. Later, she became a mother to Nana Ama Serwaah of Boankra, her only child.

Her community was part of the Asante Empire, a powerful kingdom with rich traditions, and her brother was a chief within the empire. He gave Yaa the role of Queen Mother. Part of this role was to protect the "Golden Stool"—the royal throne and great symbol of power.

Yaa took her role seriously and when the British mined the land for gold, deported Asante leaders, taxed the people, and demanded they hand over the Golden Stool, she rebelled. When the male leaders were unsure what to do, Yaa, a champion of women, notoriously declared: "...if you, the men of Asante, will not go forward, then we will. We the women will. I shall call upon my fellow women..."

After rallying the chiefs and recruiting troops, Yaa was made a war leader and her army besieged the British battalion in 1900. For months, they battled the British forces.

Despite her valiant rebellion, Yaa was eventually captured by the British and exiled to the Seychelles for the rest of her life. Although Yaa didn't live to see independence and the formation of Ghana in 1957, her legacy of leadership, dedication, and courage are commemorated through museums, schools, and awards established in her name and memory. She remains a symbol of independence and resilience today.

GHANA (ASANTE EMPIRE)

The rebellion became known as the "War of the Golden Stool" or "Yaa Asantewaa War."

U.S.A.

Some of the brothers' best-known projects include the Martin Luther King, Jr. Memorial in Washington, D.C., The National Civil Rights Museum in Memphis, Tennessee, and The Carnegie Library at Fisk University, in Nashville, Tennessee.

MOSES AND CALVIN MCKISSACK

(1879–1952 & 1890–1968)

Moses McKissack III and his brother Calvin McKissack established the first Black-owned professional architectural firm in the United States.

The seeds of the McKissack brothers' passion for building are rooted in their family history. Their grandfather, Moses McKissack I, was a Black enslaved brickmaker in Tennessee, who later gained his freedom. He had 14 children with his Cherokee Indigenous wife, Mirian. Their son, Gabriel Moses McKissack II, made his career in construction, becoming famous for his expert carpentry skills. Gabriel passed his knowledge to his sons, Moses III and Calvin.

Moses and Calvin were educated in segregated schools in Pulaski, Tennessee. By the late 1800s, Moses was working as an architect's apprentice. His reputation bloomed and soon he was building houses in Alabama and Tennessee. In 1905, Moses relocated to Nashville.

Younger brother Calvin attended Fisk University in Nashville, then worked as an architect in Texas before moving back to Nashville, too. Calvin worked with his brother, but also held different university and high school teaching posts.

In 1921, the state of Tennessee required all architects to be licensed and registered. Both Moses and Calvin completed a correspondence course in architecture from the prestigious Massachusetts Institute of Technology and became the first African Americans to take the licensing exam in 1922. The licensing authorities believed the brothers would fail because of their race, but Moses and Calvin succeeded.

They teamed-up full time and McKissack and McKissack became one of Tennessee's first registered architectural firms. Their commissions included Pearl High School, the Morris Memorial Building, and Tennessee State University's Memorial Library. Then, in 1942, the firm was hired by the US government to design and build Tuskegee Army Airfield in Alabama. At the time, the $5.7 million contract was the biggest federal contract ever awarded to a Black-owned company.

Moses and Calvin went on to become licensed in over 20 states. Moses's son William and his wife Leatrice later took on the business, and the brothers' legacy lives on through their descendants, who still build incredible architecture today!

Ann Lowe was the go-to designer for many American leaders, stars, and trendsetters of her time. Known for her artistry, she became the first internationally known African American fashion designer.

The great-granddaughter of an enslaved Black woman and a white enslaver, Ann was born into a family of seamstresses in Clayton, Alabama. Ann's mother died when she was 16, leaving her with orders to finish for important clients. Ann rose to the challenge, soon earning a name for herself.

Word of Ann's talent spread, leading her to travel to Florida to work as a dressmaker for a wealthy client. Later, she moved to New York City, where she enrolled at the S.T. Taylor Design School. Here, Ann was segregated from white students. Though her work was often used as a model of excellence in class, she often faced discrimination.

After graduating, Ann established her dress salon, designing for the rich and famous, and high-end stores. She designed and created future First Lady Jacqueline Bouvier Kennedy's iconic wedding gown.

At the time, she was given little credit, but today her designs are showcased in museums such as the Metropolitan Museum of Art and the National Museum of African American History and Culture.

ANN LOWE

(1898–1981)

U.S.A.

"All the pleasure I have had, I owe to my sewing."

Chief, teacher, and activist, Albert Luthuli made history for being the first African awarded the Nobel Peace Prize in 1960. He led millions of people in a nonviolent campaign to end apartheid in South Africa.

Albert was born in Solusi Mission Station in present-day Zimbabwe. When he was 10 years old, he and his mother moved to South Africa, where his parents were originally from. There, Albert learned the traditions of his Zulu community. After school, Albert worked as a teacher and, in 1936, he was elected as a chief of the Zulu community in Groutville, KwaZulu-Natal.

He was involved in many causes and worked to improve the lives of his fellow citizens. In 1945, he joined the African National Congress (ANC)—a political party that sought to unite African people and defend their rights. In 1948, the South African government introduced the system of apartheid. Albert became president of the ANC and campaigned against the system, leading protests and strikes.

To try to stop him, authorities arrested and accused him of treason. But Albert refused to stop and his dedication to nonviolent resistance earned him the Nobel Peace Prize. He spent the rest of his life campaigning and inspiring others.

ALBERT LUTHULI

(1898-1967)

SOUTH AFRICA

“ May the day come soon when the people of the world will rouse themselves, and together effectively stamp out any threat to peace in whatever quarter of the world it may be found. ”

Surgeon and researcher Charles Richard Drew's pioneering work on the storage of blood plasma saved lives. Charles made history as the first African American to earn a Doctor of Medical Science degree in 1940 and became the first Black surgeon elected to serve on the American Board of Surgery in 1941.

Charles spent his childhood with his parents and siblings in Washington D.C.'s Foggy Bottom. Intelligent and driven, he earned a degree from Amherst College before enrolling in medical school at Canada's McGill University. Charles next attended Columbia University where he discovered a groundbreaking technique for preserving blood. This meant blood could be stored for longer in special "blood banks."

When World War II began, Charles was asked to help supply blood to the United Kingdom where it could save the lives of the wounded. Charles got to work on the "Blood for Britain" campaign, overseeing the preservation and transportation of thousands of blood donations.

In 1941, Charles became the director of the first American Red Cross Blood Bank, but resigned in protest a year later, unable to support the then US government's baseless policy of separating blood donations by race.

Charles's legacy lives on through the countless lives saved using his research.

CHARLES DREW

(1904-1950)

" There is no scientific basis for the separation of the bloods of different races. "

U.S.A.

As the first African American to serve as a Supreme Court justice, lawyer and civil rights leader Thurgood Marshall played a critical role in confronting legal segregation in the United States and advancing equal justice for all.

Thurgood was born in Baltimore, Maryland. As a child, he was a gifted student and leader on the school debate team. Dinnertime discussions with his father helped fuel his passion for logic and law. He was also a little mischievous and, after one incident of mischief at school, he was made to memorize the entire United States Constitution!

He went on to study law at Howard University and graduated at the top of his class. He then began work for the National Association for the Advancement of Colored People (NAACP). He spent over two decades at the NAACP, arguing and winning many cases that fought racism, policies of segregation, and discrimination. His work helped to secure and defend the rights of people of color, earning him the nickname "Mr. Civil Rights."

In 1967, President Lyndon B. Johnson nominated Thurgood for the Supreme Court, the nation's highest court of justice, where he served until he retired in 1991, three years before his death.

THURGOOD MARSHALL

(1908–1993)

U.S.A.

LAW

Thurgood's legal vision was based on doing the right thing. He once said: "You do what you think is right and let the law catch up."

SISTER ROSETTA THARPE

(1915-1973)

Legendary singer and guitarist Sister Rosetta Tharpe is called "the original soul sister" and the "Godmother of rock 'n' roll" for her huge influence on music from the 1920s right up to the present day.

Rosetta was born in Cotton Plant, Arkansas, to parents who worked in the cotton fields. Her father Willis was a singer, and her mother Katie played the mandolin while singing and preaching. Little Rosetta started playing the guitar at age four.

In 1921, Rosetta's mother included her as a performer in her gospel troupe, which sang Christian music. Known as "the singing guitar-playing miracle," Rosetta crisscrossed the American South with her mother's church until they settled in Chicago. By the time she moved to New York City in the 1930s, Rosetta was becoming famous not only for her incredible musical abilities but for taking gospel music out of the church and into public places.

By age 23, Rosetta had released her first recorded song, "Rock Me," using the stage name "Sister Rosetta Tharpe." Throughout the 1940s, she recorded more hit songs and toured with fellow Black musician Marie Knight until going solo in 1951. One of her songs, "Down by

the Riverside," was chosen by the US Library of Congress' registry, a list of sound recordings deemed important for the entire country to hear.

Rosetta wowed listeners with her energetic vocals, expert electric guitar playing, and an all-new sound that formed the beginnings of rock 'n' roll. Audiences in America and Europe loved her powerful performances and joyful spirit. During a time when women electric guitarists were rare, and Black musicians faced open discrimination, Rosetta paved the way, becoming an inspiration to many people.

Rosetta died in 1973, but her music and her mark are still felt—in 1998 she was featured on a US postage stamp and in 2018 she was inducted into the Rock & Roll Hall of Fame.

66

Can't no man play like me.

99

U.S.A.

Naval Officer George Washington Gibbs Jr. was a pioneer. He became the first African American sailor to reach Antarctica, receiving the silver US Antarctic Expedition Medal.

Born in Jacksonvillle, Florida, George enlisted in the US Navy at just 19. Four years later he was selected to join an expedition to Antarctica. Due to racist policies in the US Navy at the time, the only position he could hold was "mess attendant." His duties included cooking and cleaning.

George was frustrated by his lack of options and the racism he faced, but the opportunity to set foot on the frozen lands of Antarctica was one he had to take. Throughout the expedition, George rose to every challenge and was praised for his energy and loyalty. After the expedition, George fought in World War II, surviving the torpedoing of his ship and helping others stay alive too. He left the US Navy in 1959 and went on to earn a university degree and have a successful career in business. He became a civil rights organizer and never stopped challenging unfairness and racial discrimination.

U.S.A.

Gibbs Point on the Antarctic Peninsula is named in George's honor.

JACKIE ROBINSON
(1919–1972)

Jack "Jackie" Roosevelt Robinson was the first African American to play modern Major League Baseball and become inducted into the Baseball Hall of Fame.

Jackie was born in Cairo, Georgia, but grew up in California. Money was tight and life wasn't easy for his family. Jackie's escape was sports. With his family's encouragement he pursued his passions. In high school and college, he played baseball, tennis, football, basketball, and earned medals in track-and-field events. In 1945, after a spell serving in the US army, Jackie began to play baseball for the Negro National League, but it wasn't long before his talent was noticed in the Major Leagues.

Despite facing death threats and racist heckling, he broke baseball's color barrier (the practice of excluding players of African descent) and joined the Brooklyn Dodgers in 1947, winning Rookie of the Year, gaining countless fans, and helping the Dodgers win time and again.

Jackie also dedicated his voice to civil rights activism, helping establish Black-owned businesses and speaking alongside Martin Luther King, Jr.

U.S.A.

Jackie's number, #42, was retired from the sport by the Major League in 1997 in honor of his legacy.

BERTINA LOPES
(1924–2012)

World-renowned painter and sculptor Bertina Lopes made African-inspired art using bright colors, shapes, and textures. Her work was shaped by her interest and knowledge of African folktalkes and the politics of her time.

The daughter of a Mozambican mother and Portuguese father, Bertina was born in Mozambique, which was occupied and controlled by Portugal at the time. In high school, Bertina moved to Portugal, studying with inspiring and well-known artists.

In 1953, she returned to Mozambique, teaching and painting there. During this time, many Mozambicans wanted independence from Portugal's rule, and Bertina used her art to voice her own anti-colonial and anti-discrimination views. Forced to leave her home due to her politics and associations with other figures of resistance, she relocated to Italy in 1964, where she continued to create her one-of-a-kind art until her death. She has received many awards in recognition for her work.

MOZAMBIQUE

Bertina created art for 70 years of her life. She often used her work to tell stories and express her views.

> 66
>
> *When we revolt it's not for a particular culture. We revolt simply because, for many reasons, we can no longer breathe.*
>
> 99

FRANTZ FANON (1925-1961)

Frantz Omar Fanon was a French West Indian psychiatrist and thinker whose writings explored and criticized racism and colonialism.

A descendent of enslaved Africans, Frantz was born in Martinique in the Caribbean, a French colony at the time. At 18, Frantz moved to France to fight in World War II and later studied medicine and psychiatry there. Throughout his life, Frantz experienced and witnessed racism—colonized people, Black soldiers, and everyday Black citizens were treated unjustly. Frantz wrote many books on the subject, including *Black Skin, White Masks*, and *The Wretched of the Earth*. He later moved to Algeria in Africa, another French colony, and spent his last years fighting for its independence.

Despite his short life (he died at 36), Frantz' legacy is far-reaching. He became a hero in the anti-colonial and anti-racist struggle. His work has inspired many thinkers and activists, and influenced liberation movements in Ghana, the United States, South Africa, and elsewhere.

HANS MASSAQUOI

(1926-2013)

Hans-Jürgen Massaquoi was an author, journalist, US Army paratrooper, and magazine editor. Born in Hamburg, Germany to a white German mother and a Black Liberian-Vai father, Hans was one of a tiny population of Black Germans living in Germany during World War II.

After this, Hans moved to the United States, fighting in the Korean War as a paratrooper. He later earned a journalism degree, becoming an author and editor for influential magazines that discussed and celebrated African American culture and news.

Hans wrote a memoir about his experience growing up Black in Germany when the Nazis were in power. He urged readers to fight injustice like the cruelty and racism he experienced during his youth.

> 66
>
> *It is never too soon to confront bigotry and racism whenever, wherever, and in whatever form it raises its ugly head.*
>
> 99

CORETTA SCOTT KING

(1927-2006)

Correta Scott King was an American civil rights leader who devoted her life to racial equality, gender justice, and world peace.

Coretta was born in rural Alabama and raised on the family farm. The great-granddaughter of a formerly enslaved person, Coretta was the third of four children in a family with African American, Irish, and Indigenous ancestors.

Due to laws that separated people based on their race in the American South, Coretta saw and experienced racial injustice early in life. She attended a segregated school, which she had to walk miles to get to while buses took local white children to a different school. Seeing these injustices made her want to combat racism and in college she became involved in civil rights activism.

After college, Coretta—a gifted singer—enrolled at the New England Conservatory of Music in Boston, Massachusetts, where she met and fell in love with American civil rights hero Martin Luther King, Jr.

Coretta and Martin married in 1953 and went on to have four children. Coretta and Martin shared the same goals and beliefs and campaigned together for change, social justice, and peace, until Martin was killed in 1968.

Only three weeks after her husband's assassination, Coretta addressed a crowd of thousands in New York City with an anti-war speech found in Martin's pocket on the day of his death. Coretta ensured Martin's work, words, and dreams for a better world would not be forgotten and she successfully campaigned to make Martin Luther King Jr. Day (January 16th) a national holiday in the United States.

Coretta also continued to champion causes she believed in. She protested apartheid in South Africa, actively opposed the death penalty and, in 1983, she fought to amend America's Civil Rights Act to include LGBTQ+ people.

Up until her death at 78, Coretta never stopped calling for peace and nonviolence.

> **"**
> Struggle is a never-ending process. Freedom is never really won; you earn it and win it in every generation.
> **"**

MARIAMA BÂ (1929-1981)

Mariama Bâ was a Senegalese author and women's rights activist whose books were translated into over a dozen languages.

Born in Dakar, Senegal, Mariama was raised by her grandparents in a Muslim household. As an adult she worked as a teacher before her interests in politics and the injustices she saw pushed her to write. *So Long a Letter*, her prizewinning debut novel, explores women's lives and struggles in West Africa. Her later works explored similar themes and Mariama used her voice to advocate for social change, including better education for girls.

One of the first Black African women to become globally recognized in literature, Mariama earned the Noma Award for Publishing in 1980.

Mariama is honored in Senegal today, with one of the country's top schools for girls named after her.

GLADYS MAE WEST (1930-PRESENT)

Mathematician Gladys Mae West played an instrumental role in the invention of the Global Positioning System (GPS).

Gladys was born in Sutherland, Virginia. Although she helped on the family farm, she knew early on that she wanted a different life. Education was her way out. Gladys worked hard and earned a scholarship to Virginia State College where she eventually earned a master's degree in mathematics. Gladys went on to work as a computer programmer for a naval base where she thrived for 42 years.

One achievement was her role in creating programs and collecting data that would later become GPS—a network of satellites that can be used to pinpoint the exact locations of things on Earth. A true STEM hero, Gladys was inducted into the Air Force Space and Missile Pioneers Hall of Fame in 2018.

> ❝
> I knew deep in my heart that nothing was getting in my way.
> ❞

CHINUA ACHEBE (1930–2013)

Chinua Achebe was an award-winning writer and critic. His masterwork *Things Fall Apart* has been translated into over 50 languages and sold 10 million copies since its publication in 1958.

Albert Chinualumogu Achebe, was born in the village of Ogidi on land known as the Nigeria Protectorate, occupied by the British. At school, his teachers pushed students to follow Western traditions. However, it would be the Igbo folktales, songs, and proverbs he learned as a youth that inspired his future storytelling and expressive characters. As an adult, Chinua spoke out against colonialism and his novels and writings explored African culture and the destructive impact of European occupation on African society. He remains one of Africa's best-known novelists and he is commemorated each year at the Chinua Achebe Literary Festival in Awka, the capital city of Anambra State, Nigeria.

> ❝
> If you don't like someone's story, write your own.
> ❞

ALVIN AILEY

(1931–1989)

U.S.A.

> **"**
> Dance is for everybody.
> I believe that the dance
> came from the people and
> that it should always be
> delivered back to the people.
> **"**

Visionary dancer, director, and choreographer Alvin Ailey inspired and united people through movement. His dance company was admired throughout the world for its celebration of African American culture and modern dance.

Born in rural Texas during a time of economic depression and widespread racial violence in the southern US, Alvin Ailey Jr. was raised by his mother, Lula. Life was challenging, and Lula struggled to find work. The practice of racial segregation made things harder, too. But Alvin took comfort in the sanctuary of the church. His later work was steeped in memories of the rural, Black, church-going communities where he grew up.

In 1942, Alvin moved to Los Angeles with his family. Here, he snuck out in the evenings to local dance halls to watch people dance. When he saw his first professional ballet on a high school field trip, he was truly inspired and later began taking dance lessons.

After university, Alvin performed with the Lester Horton Dance Theater, rising up to become artistic director. Soon after, Alvin moved to New York City, taking acting courses and dancing with Martha Graham (a renowned American dancer) and others. A skillful performer, he dazzled in various Broadway shows, including as the lead dancer in *Jamaica* in 1957.

In 1958, Ailey founded his own company, the Alvin Ailey American Dance Theater, one of the first companies to welcome dancers of all backgrounds. His choreography celebrated Black culture and the Black community in America. "Revelations," Alvin's masterwork, remains one of the most performed modern dance works of the 20th century. Throughout his life, he promoted arts in education, founding a dance school and junior ensemble to help bring dance to all people. Alvin died aged 58, but in 2014 he was posthumously awarded the Presidential Medal of Freedom.

MIRIAM MAKEBA

Singer, actor, and anti-apartheid activist Miriam Makeba (AKA Mama Afrika) was the first Grammy award-winning African vocalist.

Miriam was born to a Swazi mother and a Xhosa father and raised in a segregated township outside Johannesburg. Growing up, Miriam sang at church and school, and in her early twenties she joined several bands as a singer.

Whilst touring and performing in South Africa Miriam experienced and witnessed the terrible discrimination of the apartheid system.

In 1959, Miriam starred in an anti-apartheid film, which brought her international attention. Soon, she was performing in Europe and the United States. Angered by Miriam's criticism, the South African government exiled her. But Miriam had befriended many American performers, including successful Black singer-songwriter Harry Belafonte, who helped her settle in the United States and encouraged her career. Miriam continued to speak out and call for change in South Africa and became involved in civil and human rights movements around the world. Her music flourished, too. Her fusion of jazz, folk, and traditional African music was a big hit with listeners.

In 1991, after more than 30 years, Miriam returned to perform in South Africa when apartheid was ending and anti-apartheid leader Nelson Mandela asked her to come home.

SOUTH AFRICA

" I kept my culture. I kept the music of my roots. "

ANNIE EASLEY

(1933-2011)

U.S.A.

> " As my mother said, you can be anything you want to be, but you have to work at it. "

Computer scientist and mathematician Annie Easley broke down barriers in STEM. Her work helped Americans get to the Moon.

Annie was born and raised in Birmingham, Alabama. Despite segregation making it harder for Black students to access school resources,

Annie graduated at the top of her class as valedictorian. After majoring in pharmacy for a few years at university, she changed her focus to mathematics.

When Annie was hired by the National Advisory Committee for Aeronautics (later NASA) in 1955, she was one of just four Black computation staff out of 2,500 employees. For the next 34 years, she served as a vital member of

NASA's software development team. Though she had good times at work, Annie also experienced discrimination because of her skin color. She later became an equal employment opportunity counselor to help her workplace advance equality.

Annie showed other Black women that a career in STEM was achievable and her story still inspires today.

NGŨGĨ WA THIONG'O
(1938-PRESENT)

Award-winning Kenyan author, academic, and social activist Ngũgĩ wa Thiong'o, is one of East Africa's foremost literary figures.

James Thiong'o Ngũgĩ was born in Limuru, Kenya when it was a British colony. He lived through the Mau Mau Uprising (a war for independence from the British)—a subject he explored in his first novel, *Weep Not, Child*—and his painful experiences with colonialism led him to reclaim his traditional name and write in his Gikuyu Bantu language. Ngũgĩ's novels, plays, and essays often explore and critique Kenyan society and the inequalities and injustices within it. He has faced imprisonment, exile, and violence to silence him, but he continues to write and speak out.

> " Written words can also sing. "

FELA KUTI (1938-1997)

Singer and activist Fela Aníkúlápó-Kuti, AKA "Fela," was a pioneer of Afrobeat music, combining funk, jazz, and West African rhythms.

Fela was born to an affluent family in Nigeria when it was a British colony. Fela's mother, Funmilayo Ransome-Kuti, was a well-known women's rights activist, and his father was a minister. In the 1950s Fela traveled to London and enrolled at Trinity College of Music. He excelled as a trumpeter, vocalist, saxophonist, guitarist, drummer, and pianist.

On his return to Nigeria, Fela formed his band and began to tour and gain fans. Nigerian authorities detained and beat him for speaking up against cruelty and greed but he continued to use his performances to speak truth to power. When Fela died, 1 million people gathered for a funeral march to honor his memory.

> " The human spirit is stronger than any government or institution. "

JOHN LEWIS

Known as "the conscience of Congress," John Lewis was a civil rights activist and politician who served the US House of Representatives for over 30 years.

Born in rural Alabama, John attended segregated schools throughout his youth. Teenage John became inspired by Martin Luther King Jr. and met his hero at 17 years old after he was denied entry to Troy University because of his race. John eventually studied at Fisk University, earning a degree in religion and philosophy. During his student days, John joined and organized nonviolent civil rights protests, marches, and campaigns. He was one of the original Freedom Riders—a group who rode buses through Southern states in protest of segregated seating policies. John also co-led an important march for Black voter rights, which became known as "Bloody Sunday" after it ended in police violence against the peaceful marchers.

The courage he and his fellow activists showed captured worldwide attention and influenced the passage of the Voting Rights Act in 1965, meaning people could no longer be denied the right to vote due to race.

Later in life, John entered politics, where he used his position to help pass laws to make society fairer. Upon his death, the Presidential Medal of Freedom awardee was the first Black lawmaker to lie in state in the US capitol's rotunda.

USA.

" Get in good trouble, necessary trouble. "

EDMUND PETTUS BRIDGE

35

ARETHA FRANKLIN

(1942-2018)

> "We all require and want respect, man or woman, black or white. It's our basic human right."

Aretha Franklin was a singer, pianist, and songwriter. She is known as "The Queen of Soul."

Aretha Louise Franklin was born in Memphis, Tennessee but spent much of her childhood in Detroit and New York. Music was in her family. Her father, a Baptist minister, liked to sing and her mother was a gifted pianist and gospel singer. As a child, Aretha began singing in church and learned to play piano by ear. Life was sometimes hard for Aretha—her parents divorced, her mother died, and she faced many challenges, but she continued to make music.

At 18, she began to record for a broader audience, working with several record companies. In the late 1960s, she released her anthems "I Never Loved A Man" and "Respect," which catapulted her to widespread fame. Her incredible voice and mix of gospel and rhythm and blues captivated listeners. The civil rights movement was in full swing at the time and Aretha was applauded as an example of Black empowerment. She used her songs to call out for women's rights and civil rights and was asked to sing at the funeral of Martin Luther King Jr.

Aretha had many achievements, including becoming the first woman inducted into the Rock & Roll Hall of Fame in 1987, winning 18 Grammy awards, and performing at President Obama's 2009 inauguration.

ANGELA DAVIS

Activist, author, educator, and philosopher Angela Davis is one of the world's most well-known human rights advocates.

Angela Yvonne Davis was born in Alabama. She attended a segregated school and experienced racial violence and injustice. The neighborhood she lived in was frequently targeted by the Ku Klux Klan, a hate group. These experiences had an impact on young Angela and stoked her passion for civil rights. As a Girl Scout, Angela and other troop members demonstrated against segregation. In her teens, she organized study sessions for students of all races, but they were disbanded by the police. Still, she carried on.

Angela studied at several universities and went on to become a professor, teaching students philosophy and feminist studies. She was an outspoken advocate of the US Communist Party, the Black Panther Party, the feminist and Anti-Vietnam movements, the LGBTQ+ community, and the movement to abolish prisons and the death penalty. In 1970, Angela was arrested. Prosecutors alleged she was involved in a crime committed by someone she knew. Her 18-month imprisonment sparked global outcry and radically influenced her future activism. She was found not guilty of all charges and released. The bestselling author continues to write, speak, and teach today.

" You have to act as if it were possible to radically transform the world. And you have to do it all the time. "

BOB MARLEY

(1945–1981)

Jamaican singer and songwriter Bob Marley is remembered as an icon and leading figure in reggae. His music and advocacy for peace and human rights spread around the world and made him an international star.

Born in the small, rural village of Nine Mile, Robert "Bob" Nesta Marley was the son of Cedella Booker and Norval Marley. His father left the family soon after Bob's birth and died when Bob was 10 years old. Bob was harassed for being the child of an older white father and a young Black mother and nicknamed "white boy" by his bullies. His painful experiences growing up would go on to influence his thinking and his music.

Bob spent his teenage years in Trench Town, in a government-supported tenement yard in Kingston. Although conditions were brutal and violent, it was also the birthplace of reggae music, with Bob as one of its pioneers. During this time, Bob explored different music genres (including ska), worked on his singing skills, and released songs. In 1963, he created The Wailers, a ska and reggae group with friends Peter Tosh and Bunny Wailer. The band, led by Marley's distinct voice, found success from the start and continued to grow and gain international fame.

A believer in anti-colonialism, anti-racism, and equal human rights, Bob used his music to share his ideas. When The Wailers split in 1974, Bob launched his solo career, with many of his songs promoting peace and love as well as highlighting oppression. His power was feared by some and, in 1976, he survived an assassination attempt. He continued to use his voice and, in 1978, Bob tried to help unite battling political groups in Jamaica by headlining the "One Love" concert.

After his death from cancer at age 36, Bob was honored with the Jamaican government's Order of Merit and laid to rest by thousands of mourners, who visited while he laid in state in Jamaica's National Arena. Decades after his death, Bob's music continues to move listeners old and new, and his legacy of striving for peace and unity is not forgotten.

JAMAICA

> 66
>
> Get up, stand
> up, stand up for
> your right. Get up,
> stand up, don't
> give up the fight.
>
> 99

OCTAVIA BUTLER (1947-2006)

Award-winning author Octavia Butler was a visionary writer of the science-fiction genre. Her books explored race, gender, women's rights, and climate change.

Octavia was born in Pasadena, California. A very shy girl, she lived with dyslexia, a learning difference that affects how our brains process language. Despite this, she found solace in reading and writing, and in the sci-fi genre most of all.

Octavia is best known for her books *Kindred*, *Fledgling*, *Patternmaster*, and *Parable of the Sower*. In addition to many awards given for her masterful writing, Octavia was also the first science-fiction writer to be awarded a MacArthur Genius Grant. Her fanbase continues to grow after her death, with new readers discovering her words.

" I began writing about power because I had so little. "

THOMAS SANKARA

(1949-1987)

Thomas Sankara was Burkina Faso's president for just four years, but his revolutionary politics established him as an iconic African leader.

Thomas was born in Yako, Upper Volta, a French colony at the time. He pursued a career in the military and soon rose up the ranks. His interest in progressive politics and his frustration with the poverty and corruption he saw led him to pursue a position of power, where he could bring about change.

After a coup, Thomas became president at age 33. He renamed the country Burkina Faso—"the land of upright people"—and quickly set about making positive changes for women's rights, healthcare, literacy, the environment, and much more. His time in power was cut short when he was assassinated, but his visionary work lives on.

BURKINA FASO

> "While revolutionaries as individuals can be murdered, you cannot kill ideas."

IMAN (1955-PRESENT)

World-famous supermodel, actor, entrepreneur, and philanthropist Iman is known for breaking barriers in fashion and business.

The daughter of a Somalian diplomat, Iman Abdulmajid was born into a middle-class Muslim family in present-day Somalia. After her family were forced to leave their homeland as refugees, Iman studied political science at university in Nairobi, Kenya. There, she was spotted by American photographer Peter Beard, who noticed her incredible beauty and spirit. With Beard's help, Iman moved to the United States and quickly became one of the world's most influential and sought-after fashion models. She was featured in magazines and became the muse of many designers, inspiring future diverse models. She branched out into TV and movies, started her own cosmetics line, and married rock star David Bowie. Today, she is also known for her charity work and for championing important causes, including education.

> "The day you settle for less is the day you will get less."

A masterful composer, producer, singer, songwriter, and multi-instrumentalist, Prince was one of the most exceptional musicians of his era and beyond.

Born in Minneapolis, Minnesota, Prince Rogers Nelson was the son of accomplished musicians. His mother Mattie was a jazz singer and his father John was a songwriter and pianist. He developed his passion for music early on and learned how to play the drums, piano, and guitar.

Music and dance were a source of joy and escape for Prince growing up. He mixed with other young musicians from Minneapolis, performed in bands, and worked as a guitarist. By age 18 he signed a contract with a major record label, Warner Records, and his career took off.

He released a new album every year, earning a name for himself amongst critics. In 1984, he released his sixth album, *Purple Rain* and made his acting debut in a dramatic rock musical of the same name. Both the movie and the album were huge successes. Prince soon became an international star and whenever he took the stage, he would wow the audience with his iconic style, genre-bending sound, stage-presence, and distinct voice. He became known for breaking boundaries and labels and was loved for his rebellious style. After becoming frustrated with his record label's control, he even changed his name to a symbol (see purple symbol on opposite page), becoming known as "The Artist Formerly Known as Prince" for several years.

Alongside his unique talent, Prince was also celebrated for his powerful partnerships and promotion of other artists in both music and movies, as well as for his activism, animal rights advocacy, and charitable work.

A Rock & Roll Hall of Fame inductee, Grammy Award winner, and Academy Award winner, Prince was named one of *Rolling Stone Magazine*'s "100 Greatest Artists of All Time." Selling over 100 million albums during his lifetime, and many more after his death in 2016, he remains one of the world's bestselling artists.

> "If I'm going to do something I'm going to do it well."

OZWALD BOATENG
(1967–PRESENT)

Fashion designer, tailor, and entrepreneur Ozwald Boateng is famous for his signature style and artistry.

Ozwald was born in London to Ghanaian parents, who moved to England from Ghana in the 1950s. His mother was a seamstress, so Ozwald was introduced to clothes-making from an early age. He went on to study fashion design at Southgate College and in his early twenties Ozwald used his mother's old sewing machine to create his first clothing collection, which he sold to a London menswear store.

Ozwald's star continued to rise. He dressed celebrities, became the first tailor to host a catwalk show at Paris Fashion Week, and the youngest tailor to open a shop on Savile Row (a street in London famous for its tailors). His iconic blend of classic tailoring and bold colors shook up the men's fashion industry.

For over 25 years Ozwald's hard work and creativity earned him many awards, honors, and opportunities, but Ozwald also gave back, championing investment in African businesses and ideas.

Today, Ozwald continues to design incredible clothes for runways, TV, movies, and more.

MARCUS SAMUELSSON
(1971-PRESENT)

Marcus Samuelsson is an award-winning chef with restaurants around the world.

Born in Ethiopia, Marcus and his sister Fantaye were separated from their family during the Ethiopian Civil War in 1974. The siblings were adopted by a Swedish family and raised in Gothenberg, Sweden. There, Marcus was introduced to the art of cooking by his Swedish grandmother. His fascination with food led to cookery school, a move to the United States, rave reviews, awards, cook books, TV appearances, and one-of-a-kind opportunities, including cooking for President Obama's first state dinner. One of Marcus's most famous restaurants is Red Rooster in Harlem, New York. Marcus also invests time in helping underserved communities, and believes everyone has a right to good food.

SWEDEN

ETHIOPIA

" Hard work IS its own reward. Integrity IS priceless. Art DOES feed the soul. "

LEYMAH GBOWEE
(1972-PRESENT)

Peace activist Leymah Gbowee is the second African woman to win the Nobel Peace Prize for her work leading the Women of Liberia Mass Action for Peace movement.

Leymah was born and raised in central Liberia. At just 17, her life changed when the First Liberian Civil War broke out. After a period in Ghana as a refugee, she returned to Liberia, where she trained in trauma counseling and worked with former child soldiers. Leymah knew women could be a force for change. She rallied women from different faiths to unite in nonviolent protests, which helped bring peace. Leymah's story has earned her many awards and inspired a documentary. She continues to champion peace and women's empowerment today.

LIBERIA

" I'm never afraid to speak truth to power. "

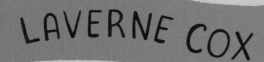

(1972-PRESENT)

Famous for her award-winning acting and activism, trailblazing Laverne Cox was the first openly transgender woman of color to lead a TV series.

Laverne was born in Mobile, Alabama and raised with her identical twin by her mother and her grandmother. Growing up, Laverne knew she was a girl. She was bullied because of her gender identity, but despite pressures from some of her peers to conform to their ideas about who she should be, Laverne stayed true to herself.

She studied creative writing and classical ballet in college, before moving to New York City and focusing on acting. Laverne spent years working on her craft, acting in shows and on TV. In 2012, she was cast in her breakout role as a transgender prison inmate in the hit Netflix drama *Orange Is the New Black*. The role would launch Laverne into stardom.

Laverne proudly advocates for LGBTQ+ rights and has established a track record for breaking barriers and opening doors in the entertainment industry for future transgender stars.

> " We are not what other people say we are. We are who we know ourselves to be, and we are what we love. That's okay. "

PHOEBE ROBINSON

(1984–PRESENT)

Multitalented comedian, podcaster, producer, actor, and best-selling author Phoebe Robinson is known for her relatable humor and powerful storytelling that amplifies and celebrates diverse voices.

Phoebe grew up in the suburbs of Cleveland, Ohio. She attended a private Catholic high school where she was the only Black girl in her graduating class. She dreamed of writing movies and, after high school, she moved to New York City, majoring in screenwriting at Pratt Institute. Following college, Phoebe wrote for TV shows, blogged, and podcasted. She started to perform stand-up comedy, talking to audiences about things she cared about and found funny. Phoebe then met fellow Black comic and actor Jessica Williams and, in 2016, they developed 2 Dope Queens, a popular podcast (later turned into a TV series) that centered around their friendship and gave a platform to other comedians of color.

Phoebe's meteoric rise didn't end there. She has created more solo podcasts, starred in movies, written books, launched her own production company, and continues to make people laugh with her comedy.

LOL!

" You have the power to dictate your own life. "

You can knock me down, but I get up twice as strong.

LEWIS HAMILTON

(1985-PRESENT)

Prizewinning Formula One (F1) racing driver and seven-time World Champion Lewis Hamilton is the first Black driver to win the F1 World Drivers' Championship.

Born in Stevenage, England into a multiracial Roman Catholic family with a white British mother and a Black father of Grenadian origins, Lewis Carl Davidson Hamilton was named after Black American Olympic track and fielder Carl Lewis.

In 1991, Lewis's father gifted him a remote-control car, which sparked his interest in racing. He started out racing karts at age eight. A hard worker with natural talent, Lewis soon reached the top of go-kart racing and by the time he was 10, he had won Britain's cadet karting competition. But Lewis wasn't close to finished. He had a big goal in his sights—becoming an F1 driver.

At 13, Lewis signed with the McLaren and Mercedes-Benz Young Driver Support Program, taking his racing to the next level. Two years later, he was the youngest racer in history to earn the kart racing's number-one position. Then, in 2007, he made his hard-earned debut as an F1 driver for McLaren and became the first driver with Black ancestry to compete in the series. His career has been at full speed ever since, with Lewis winning races, breaking records, and gaining fans worldwide.

In addition to his seven World Drivers' Championship wins, over the years Lewis has gone on to claim the most F1 wins, podium finishes, and pole positions—making him the most successful British F1 driver in history.

Lewis also makes moves off the track. He has spoken out against racism and the lack of diversity in motorsports, often using his platform to call out injustice. His charity, Mission 44 (named after his racing number), seeks to help young people from underrepresented backgrounds.

UNITED KINGDOM

> "Write the tale that scares you, that makes you feel uncertain, that isn't comfortable. I dare you."

MICHAELA COEL

(1987-PRESENT)

Michaela Coel made history as the first Black woman to win an Emmy award for outstanding writing for a limited series.

Michaela Ewuraba Boakye-Collinson was born in London to Ghanaian parents. She grew up with her mother and sister on a council estate. The family experienced poverty, but Michaela loved many aspects of her childhood. In her late teens, she began performing poetry at open mic nights. She enrolled at the Guildhall School of Music and Drama in London, where she wrote the play *Chewing Gum Dreams*, inspired by her experiences growing up. The play's success led to the award-winning TV series *Chewing Gum*, which Michaela wrote and starred in. Her next series, *I May Destroy You*, brought her international fame and led to her history-making Emmy award.

Michaela continues to write, act, and direct. Her work often tells stories of "misfits" and people who feel on the outside of society.

U.S.A.

"To me, this is bigger than football and it would be selfish on my part to look the other way."

COLIN KAEPERNICK

(1987-PRESENT)

Colin "Kap" Kaepernick is an American football quarterback and social justice activist.

Colin was born in Milwaukee, Wisconsin and adopted and raised by Rick and Teresa Kaepernick. The Kaepernick family moved to California when Colin was four years old.

Growing up, Colin was very athletic. At high school, he excelled in many sports including football, basketball, and baseball. But Colin's passion was football, and he earned a football scholarship at the University of Nevada. His talent shone and in 2011 after graduating college, he was selected by the San Francisco 49ers. He flourished on the team for several seasons.

In 2016, Colin made history when he decided to protest police brutality and racism by kneeling during the US national anthem prior to each game of the season. Colin faced criticism and threats to his career, but many people were inspired and joined in, kneeling in solidarity. Today, Colin continues to pursue football and champion causes that help fight inequalities in society.

KADEENA COX

(1991-PRESENT)

> 66
> *You just have to
> have heart, passion,
> determination and
> self-belief.*
> 99

Famed four-time Paralympic gold medalist Kadeena Cox is the first British Black athlete to win a gold medal in either Olympic or Paralympic cycling.

Kadeena Cox is the daughter of Jamaican parents, Asmond and Jasmin. She grew up with 11 siblings in Leeds in the United Kingdom. As a child, Kadeena was active and brave. She cycled from a young age and was drawn to sports and dance. Her competitive sprinting career kicked off at age 15 when her field hockey coach saw her talent and encouraged her to run. Over the next five years, Kadeena trained and competed, winning races and earning a name for herself. Between training and competing, Kadeena also enrolled at Manchester Metropolitan University, where she studied physiotherapy.

Kadeena's life took a new path in 2014 after she had a stroke, which led to her being diagnosed with multiple sclerosis, a disease which affects the nervous system. Kadeena moved forward and developed new ambitions.

In 2015, Kadeena launched her Paralympic career and, in 2016, at the Paralympics in Rio de Janeiro, Brazil, Kadeena made history as the first British Paralympian in 32 years to win gold medals in two sports (athletics and cycling) at a single edition of the Paralympic Games.

Kadeena's razor-sharp dedication to her goals has led her to success after success. She has set world records in both sports, won medals, and inspired fans around the world. In 2017, she was awarded an MBE (Member of the Order of the British Empire) and, in 2022, an OBE (Order of the

British Empire) after winning two more gold medals at the 2020 Tokyo Olympics in Japan.

Alongside her sporting achievements, Kadeena has used her platform to speak out on issues close to her heart, such as body image and racism. In 2021, she founded KC Academy, an organization that is working to increase diversity in elite cycling by providing funding, support, and mentorship to diverse athletes.

AISHA DEE (1993-PRESENT)

Actor Aisha Dee was born on the Australian Gold Coast to an African American father and a white Australian mother.

As a little girl, Aisha grew up in a mainly white, conservative area. She loved watching *Sesame Street* and Hollywood movies from the 1970s. The diversity of the actors she saw onscreen encouraged her own dreams of acting.

At 16, Aisha moved to California, finding success as a teen actor on the Australian-Canadian series, *The Saddle Club*. Her star continued to rise and, in 2016, she was cast as Kat Edison on *The Bold Type*, a comedy-drama series that earned her rave reviews and many more fans. She is passionate about encouraging diversity both onscreen and behind the scenes in the TV and movie industry.

> " I'm hopeful we will have the opportunity to tell more authentic stories by hiring, promoting, and listening to diverse voices. "

ADENIKE OLADOSU
(1994-PRESENT)

Adenike Oladosu is an award-winning climate activist and ecofeminist who launched the Fridays for Future Nigeria climate strike.

Adenike was born in Abuja, Nigeria. After school, she studied agricultural economics at university. She joined the environmental justice movement, calling for change and action to protect the planet. Her interest in ecofeminism was sparked after terrorist group, Boko Haram, abducted schoolgirls in Nigeria. She believed there was a link between this kidnapping and the drying out of Lake Chad, which devastated the area and led to more poverty and crime.

Adenike has spoken at global conferences about how climate injustice increases the displacement and harming of people across Africa. She has launched a movement to restore Lake Chad and is passionate about inspiring younger generations.

> " Becoming an activist is more than a choice for me, it's a necessity "

NAOMI OSAKA

(1997–PRESENT)

Professional tennis powerhouse Naomi Osaka's groundbreaking 2018 US Open win made her Japan's first Grand Slam Singles competition winner.

Naomi was born in Osaka, Japan to a Haitian father and a Japanese mother. When she was three, her family moved to Long Island, New York, where her father began training both Naomi and her sister Mari to play tennis. The girls were homeschooled at night so they could train during the day. In 2013, Naomi went pro, representing Japan, and soon skyrocketed through the tennis ranks. A year after her 2018 win, her fierce and skillful performance saw her win the Australian Open, and become the first Asian player to be ranked number 1 in the world in singles tennis.

Known for her will to speak up about injustices, in 2020 at the US Open, Naomi donned seven face masks, one for each of her tennis matches, with the names of African Americans killed by racial violence. Beyond tennis, Naomi has branched out into fashion, skin care, and other businesses, inspiring others with her hard work and success.

"
You just gotta keep going and fighting for everything, and one day you'll get to where you want.
"

JAPAN

U.S.A.

AMANDA GORMAN

Poetic phenom, spoken word artist, and activist Amanda Gorman is the first person to be named National Youth Poet Laureate of the United States. She made history as the youngest inaugural poet in the nation's history when she recited her poem "The Hill We Climb" at President Joe Biden's 2021 inauguration.

Amanda was raised by her mother, a middle-school teacher, with her siblings, in the Watts neighborhood in Los Angeles. Amanda experienced challenges with speech and struggled to pronounce the letter "r" due to an auditory processing condition affecting how people register what they hear. Poetry became an accessible way for Amanda to express herself.

Despite the frustrations of having some people mistake her accent due to her speech impediment, Amanda found ways to work on her speech that brought her joy, including listening to songs she loved on repeat. She also gained inspiration to use her voice by wearing a necklace from her ancestor Amanda, a formerly enslaved person who could not read or write. Wearing her namesake's jewelry helped her soothe her nerves and gain confidence.

Inspired by Nobel Prize laureate Malala Yousafzai's global social change work, Amanda joined the United Nations Youth Delegate Programme in 2013 and later spoke at the UN Summit. By age 16, she had been selected to be the first Youth Poet Laureate of Los Angeles and published a poetry collection. Two years later, she founded One Pen One Page, an organization offering free creative writing programs for underprivileged youth.

Amanda gained worldwide recognition after sharing her words at President Joe Biden's inauguration in 2021. New readers and listeners around the globe were introduced to her poetry, which explores social justice issues such as race, feminism, and climate change. Just one month later, she accomplished another first—reciting the first-ever original poem at the Super Bowl.

Today, Amanda holds a degree in sociology from Harvard University and continues to make her mark as an author, poet, fashion model, and social justice advocate.

There is always light. If only we were brave enough to see it. If only we're brave enough to be it.

CHLOE X HALLE

Sister songstresses Chloe and Halle Bailey have achieved fame and success as musical duo Chloe x Halle. The innovative and collaborative pair are known for breaking barriers in both music and cinema.

Born Chloe Elizabeth Bailey and Halle Lynn Bailey, the sisters grew up in Mableton, Georgia, near Atlanta. Noticing their interest in music, their father started helping the sisters learn about songwriting when they were 10 and 8. Soon, they were writing their own tunes and learning to play instruments by watching online tutorials.

When Chloe and Halle were 13 and 11, they started their YouTube channel, posting videos of them singing covers of other musicians' songs. The duo's big breakthrough happened when superstar singer Beyonce watched their cover of her song, "Pretty Hurts." Soon, the sisters were signed to Beyonce's record label and being mentored by the superstar.

After a few years of making music and touring, Chloe x Halle released their debut album *The Kids Are Alright* in 2018. The album earned the sisters their first two Grammy award nominations, including Best New Artist. Their album *Ungodly Hour* followed in 2020. It was another success and helped the sisters win the 2020 Billboard Women in Music Rising Star Award. The sisters' music is a blend of their tastes and a mix of music genres, including R&B, pop, and soul.

Alongside their music career together, multitalented Chloe and Halle also act. Between 2017 and 2022 the sisters both appeared in the TV series *Grown-ish* for four seasons. Chloe and Halle have found success as individuals, too. Chloe has released music as a solo artist and been cast in several movies, while in 2019 Halle was cast as Princess Ariel in a live-action remake of Disney's *The Little Mermaid*.

The creative sisters often use their voices to speak out for causes they believe in, including racial justice and encouraging younger generations to vote.

> " We will continue to use our platforms for the little black girls and boys, to show them they can do this, and when they see proper representation, they'll believe in themselves more. "

"Justice is all we've ever wanted, and music has been healing since the beginning of our lives."

U.S.A.

NTANDO MAHLANGU
(2002-PRESENT)

Sprinter and long jumper Ntando Mahlangu is a record-breaking Paralympic athlete.

Ntando was born in Mpumalanga, South Africa, with fibular hemimelia, which stopped his legs from developing below the knee. Ntando used a wheelchair until he was 10 years old, when he was fitted for his first "running blade" prosthetics, thanks to a local charity called Jumping Kids. From then on Ntando began to run and race.

By 14, Ntando won silver in the 200m at the Rio de Janeiro 2016 Paralympic Games. He has been breaking records ever since, winning two medals at the World Para Athletics Championships, and two gold medals at the Tokyo 2020 Paralympics. In Netflix documentary *Rising Phoenix* Ntando is seen racing a cheetah!

" ...I've learned to fly. I've learned to run and to be myself. "

ZAILA AVANT-GARDE
(2007-PRESENT)

Lover of books, math, and basketball, Zaila Avant-garde became the first African American winner of the Scripps National Spelling Bee in 2021, aged just 14.

Born in Harvey, Louisiana, Zaila developed a passion for books from a young age. Her love of reading influenced her rise into competitive spelling. She also found inspiration from a Guinness book her parents gave her for her eighth birthday. The book of amazing achievements motivated her to earn three basketball juggling world records by age 12. Zaila's willingness to challenge herself and pursue multiple interests and dreams is an inspiration to many children around the world.

Multitalented Zaila has voiced two main goals for her future, so far: to work for NASA, and to play basketball for the WNBA.

MARI COPENY
(2007–PRESENT)

Activist and philanthropist Mari Copeny captured her country's attention at just eight years old when she saw a problem in her community and used her voice to speak up.

Born in Flint, Michigan, it would be Mari's hometown that first put her on the map. In 2014, Flint's local government changed the city's water source but failed to ensure the new water supply was safe. Residents noticed the drinking water seemed different. Testing showed high levels of lead in the water. Thousands of Flint residents were being exposed to dangerous drinking water.

Young Mari felt she had to act. In 2015 she sent President Barack Obama a letter about the crisis, introducing herself as "Little Miss Flint." Her words inspired him and raised awareness around the country. Obama traveled to Flint to see the problem and authorized $100 million in funding to help.

Since then, Mari has continued to call for change for her community and others. She has spoken at marches, raised funds for schoolchildren, and partnered with a company to produce a water filter so that people like the Flint residents can drink safely.

> *We need to protect dreamers, we need to protect kids in the most vulnerable areas, we need love and for people to care about their communities.*

GLOSSARY

Abolitionist movement An organized effort to end slavery. There have been abolitionist movements in countries around the world, including the UK and the US.

Activist Someone who campaigns for social change.

Advocate Someone who supports or champions a cause, idea, or action.

AKA An acronym that stands for "also known as."

Apartheid A legal, political, and cultural system in South Africa from 1948 to the 1990s. It was designed to separate people according to their race and ethnicity.

Architecture Designing and constructing buildings and other structures. An architect is someone who does this as their job.

Autobiographical Based on the writer's own life or experiences.

Bigotry Having strong, unreasonable views and intolerance of differing views.

Bullying A repeated behavior such as teasing and name calling, intended to hurt someone.

Civil rights The rights every human has to be free and equal.

Climate change A long-term change in the planet's average weather and temperature patterns.

Colonialism The process of one country taking control of another country or area and its people in order to gain more power, land, and resources.

Colony A country or area that is controlled by another country.

Conform To be or act in agreement with something.

Council estate A housing development in the UK built by a local authority and provided for people on lower incomes.

Coup A sudden overthrow of an existing government.

Culture The arts and ideas of a community.

Discrimination Unfair treatment of people based on characteristics such as race, age, or gender.

Ecofeminism A type of feminism that explores connections between the oppression of women and ecological concerns such as climate change.

Emmy Award An American award given to actors, directors, and other TV professionals by the Academy of Television Arts and Sciences. There are many different categories and new winners are chosen each year.

Entrepreneur Someone who creates their own business and takes responsibility for its successes and losses.

Equality Being equal in rights and opportunities.

Exile When someone is forced to leave or refused re-entry to their country.

Feminism The belief in social, economic, cultural, and political equality of people of all genders.

Folk A music genre based on the traditional music of a country, area, or people. Characteristics include acoustic instruments (not electric) such as guitar and fiddle, and storytelling lyrics.

Gender identity Someone's personal sense and experience of their own gender.

Gospel A music genre characterized by strong vocals, hymn-like melodies, and spiritual lyrics based on Christianity.

Grammy Award An American award given by the American National Academy of Recording Arts and Sciences to recognize achievement in the music industry. There are many different categories and new winners are chosen each year.

Guerrilla tactics Actions performed in a sudden, unpredictable way, usually by small groups during a war or conflict.

Human rights Basic rights and freedoms that belong to every person in the world.

Icon Someone who is greatly admired, represents a particular idea, or has a big influence in a particular field.

Jazz A music genre first developed by Black American musicians in the early 1900s. Characteristics include improvisation and brass wind instruments such as trumpet.

LGBTQ+ An acronym that stands for Lesbian, Gay, Bisexual, Transgender, Queer or Questioning and plus, which represents other identities.

Lie in state A tradition where the body of someone who has died (usually an important person) is placed in a coffin in a public place so that people can view it and show their respect.

Muse Someone who is a source of inspiration for an artist, writer, designer, musician, or other creative person.

Myriad Countless or very great in number.

Nazis Members of a far-right German political party that was in power between 1933 and 1945. Nazi policies were antisemitic (prejudiced and oppressive against Jewish people), racist, and deeply discriminatory and violent.

Nobel Prize   An annual international prize awarded to people who have made outstanding contributions to the world. There are prizes for various fields including science, literature, economics, and the promotion of peace.

Noble   Someone who belongs to the highest rank or class in a society.

Olympian   An athlete who competes or has competed in the Olympic Games (an international multi-sports competition that happens every four years).

Open mic night   An event, usually at night, at which anyone in the audience is allowed to perform by telling jokes, reciting poetry, singing, and so on.

Oppression   When a person or group in power controls another person or group through force, cruelty, or other unfair measures.

Paralympian   An athlete who competes or has competed in the Paralympic Games (an international multi-sports competition for people with disabilities that happens every four years).

Phenom   Someone who is extremely successful, talented, or admired.

Philanthropy   Helping other people usually through donating money or other resources. Someone who practices philanthropy is a philanthropist.

Plantation   A large farm on which a particular crop, such as cotton, is grown.

Pop   A music genre that is designed to appeal to a wide audience. Characteristics include electronic instruments, memorable lyrics, strong rhythm, and short songs.

Poverty   When someone does not have enough money and resources to afford and access basic needs such as food or shelter.

Prosthetic   A mobility device that is used in place of a missing body part to help the person move and function.

Psychiatry   A field of medicine that involves mental health conditions. A doctor who works in psychiatry is called a psychiatrist.

R&B (rhythm & blues)   A music genre that was developed by Black Americans in the 1940s. Characteristics include keyboards and smooth vocals.

Racism   Treating a person or group unjustly on the basis of their race. Racism occurs between individuals and operates within social and political systems.

Refugee   Someone who has been forced to leave their country, often because of a war or another threatening event.

Reggae   A music genre that developed in Jamaica. Characteristics include social and political lyrics, offbeat rhythms, and percussion instruments.

Rock 'n' roll   A music genre developed in the 1950s in the United States. Characteristics include electric guitar, fast tempos, drums, and energetic performances.

Sanctuary   A safe place.

Science-fiction (sci-fi)   Books or movies about imaginary future events, often involving space travel and future technology.

Segregation   Separating people into different groups based on skin color.

Ska   A music genre developed in Jamaica in the late 1950s that combines traditional Caribbean music and jazz. Characteristics include fast tempo and use of brass wind instruments such as saxophone.

Slavery   When someone is treated as property by someone else and forced to work for them. An enslaver is someone who owns enslaved people.

Slave trade   The business or practice of enslaving, transporting, selling, and buying human beings.

Social justice   The belief that all humans deserve equal rights and opportunities.

Solace   Something that brings comfort in a time of sadness or distress.

Soul   A music genre developed by Black Americans in the 1960s. Characteristics include touches of gospel and R&B and emphasis on vocals and meaningful lyrics.

Stand-up comedy   When a comedian performs onstage in front of a live audience, speaking directly to the audience.

Township   A residential area in South Africa, usually on the outskirts of towns and cities, reserved for people of color to live in during apartheid to keep them segregated from white people.

Transatlantic slave trade   A segment of the global slave trade that occurred between 1500 and 1900. It involved Europeans enslaving and transporting many millions of Africans across the Atlantic Ocean, to forcibly work for white people in Europe, the Americas, and the Caribbean.

Transgender   Someone whose gender identity is different to the sex they were assigned at birth.

Treason   When someone tries to overthrow their country's government, often by working with their country's enemies.

Underprivileged   A person or group who have fewer advantages and opportunities—such as education and wealth—than average.

Underrepresented   A person or group who do not have enough people in positions of power to speak for them, help them, or inspire them.

Underserved   A person or group who have limited access to or face barriers accessing goods and services.

Verse   Poetry or writing that is arranged in a rhythmic pattern.

To Pedro, always be your full self.—A.P.

To Mom and your infinite and everloving spirit. You remain my all-time favorite
"Well-Read Black Girl."
To Dad, my very first editor. Thanks for introducing me to Pushkin and beyond.
To Travis, thank you for the music and more.—J.W.

Brimming with creative inspiration, how-to projects, and useful information to enrich your everyday life, Quarto is a favorite destination for those pursuing their interests and passions. Visit our site and dig deeper with our books into your area of interest: Quarto Creates, Quarto Cooks, Quarto Homes, Quarto Lives, Quarto Drives, Quarto Explores, Quarto Gifts, or Quarto Kids.

Young, Gifted and Black, Too © 2023 Quarto Publishing plc.
Text © 2023 Jamia Wilson.
Illustrations © 2023 Andrea Pippins.

First published in 2023 by Wide Eyed Editions, an imprint of The Quarto Group.
100 Cummings Center, Suite 265D, Beverly, MA 01915 USA.
T +1 978-282-9590 F+1 978-283-2742 **www.Quarto.com**

The right of Andrea Pippins to be identified as the illustrator and Jamia Wilson to be identified
as the author of this work has been asserted by them in accordance with the Copyright, Designs
and Patents Act, 1988 (United Kingdom).

A CIP record for this book is available from the Library of Congress.

ISBN 978-0-7112-7702-1
eISBN 978-0-7112-7701-4

The illustrations were created in ink and colored digitally
Set in Futura, Buttacup Lettering, and Azaelia

Published by Debbie Foy and Georgia Amson-Bradshaw • Designed by Karissa Santos
Edited by Hannah Dove • Production by Dawn Cameron

Manufactured in Guangdong, China TT112022

9 8 7 6 5 4 3 2 1